Caligulan

CALIGULAN

Poems by
Ernest Hilbert

Measure Press
Evansville, Indiana

The text of this book is composed in Baskerville.
Composition by R.G.
Cover design by Jennifer Mercer.
Cover and author photographs by Matthew Wright.
Manufacturing by Ingram.

Hilbert, Ernest
 Caligulan / by Ernest Hilbert—1st ed.

 ISBN-13: 978-1-939574-13-8
 ISBN-10: 1-939574-13-7
 Library of Congress Control Number: 2015914406

In the spirit of E.F. Benson, author of the chilling tale "The Room in the Tower," the present author fervently wishes his readers a few uncomfortable moments.

Measure Press
526 S. Lincoln Park Dr.
Evansville, IN 47714

I extend many thanks to the editors of the magazines in which these poems originally appeared, including *Academic Questions*, *American Arts Quarterly*, *American Poetry Review*, *Apiary*, *Asheville Poetry Review*, *At Length*, *Battersea Review*, *Birmingham Poetry Review*, *B O D Y*, *Boston Review*, *Clarion* (Boston Poetry Union), *Cleaver*, *Dark Horse*, *Edinburgh Review*, *Fruita Pulp*, *Hopkins Review*, *Hudson Review*, *Measure*, *Parnassus*, *Philadelphia Inquirer*, *Listen: Life with Classical Music*, *New Dublin Press*, *New Criterion*, *Raintown Review*, *Smartish Pace*, *Yale Review*, and *2 Bridges Review*.

A recording of Ernest Hilbert reading "Broad and Washington," engineered by Peter Crimmins, was broadcast on WHYY/NPR 90.7FM as part of the News Works Tonight New Year's program the evening of December 31, 2013. "*Atlantica*" appeared in autumn 2014 as a limited-edition broadside poster from Lithic Press. "Judgement" is the name of a band, and it is dedicated to all of its members. "Insomnia Redux" borrows its title from an orchestral piece by composer Daniel Felsenfeld. "Barnegat Light" is in memory of Stephen Berg. "Watchers" is for Russell Davis, who inspired its theme and progress. "Kite" is for David Yezzi. "Mineral Point" is for Benjamin Longfellow. Special thanks to Sunil Iyengar for etymological expertise and guidance.

The evolution of this collection from earliest draft to final publication has been influenced at every stage by astute suggestions offered and fierce objections raised by Bill Coyle, David Yezzi, and Justin Quinn. I owe immense gratitude to photographer Matthew Wright for scouting and setting up in the dead of winter at an abandoned factory, confronting surly representatives of the Federal Railroad Administration with such insouciance, and eluding local police with such nimbleness.

Thanks most especially to my wife, Lynn, my first reader, and all her family, my family and friends, everyone at Measure Press, everyone at Bauman Rare Books, as well as anyone, enemy or ally, I have, in my selfishness, forgotten.

The epigraph to "Watchers" can be found in Juvenal's notorious sixth satire, typically translated as "who will guard the guardians?" The epigraph to "Light Illumined" is from Canto XXVI of Dante's *Purgatorio*, translated by Allen Mandelbaum as "While we moved at the edge, one first, one after, / and I could

often hear my gentle master / saying: 'Take care—and do not waste my warning.'"
The book's epigraph, from Suetonius' *De vita Caesarum*, is translated by J.C. Rolfe
as "[Caligula] seldom had anyone put to death except by numerous slight wounds,
his constant order, which soon became well-known, being: 'Strike so that he may
feel that he is dying.' When a different man than he had intended had been killed,
through a mistake in the names, he said that the victim too had deserved the same
fate. He often uttered the familiar line of the tragic poet [Lucius Accius]: 'Let
them hate me, so they but fear me.'"

CONTENTS

Summer

Autumn

Winter

Spring

Non temere in quemquam nisi crebris et minutis ictibus animadverti passus est, perpetuo notoque iam praecepto: "Ita feri ut se mori sentiat." Punito per errorem nominis alio quam quem destinaverat, ipsum quoque paria meruisse dixit. Tragicum illud subinde iactantibus: "Oderint, dum metuant."

— Suetonius

Caligulan

Adjective   ca·li·gu·lan   \kə-'li-gyə-lən\

Of, pertaining to, or evoking one or more of the following states, often co-occurring:

- Illogical fear that disaster, especially of a gruesome kind, might befall one at any time;
- Constant worry for the safety of oneself and one's loved ones; and/or;
- Obsession with cruel and irrational behavior.

The condition denotes:

1. a: painful or apprehensive uneasiness of mind over a seemingly impending ill;

b: fearful concern or morbid interest in human degradation or capricious acts of violence;

c: sensations akin to those experienced by Roman citizens, nobles, and senators, as well as immediate family members of the emperor, during the brief but profoundly sadistic reign of the Roman emperor Caligula, Gaius Julius Caesar Augustus Germanicus (31 August AD 12 to 24 January AD 41), emperor (AD 37 to 41);

d: an abnormal and overwhelming sense of apprehension, dread, and fear, often marked by physiological signs (such as profuse sweating, increased pulse rate, sleeplessness, sensation of phantom third limbs, and marked increase in alcohol consumption), by doubts concerning the reality and nature of an unspecified threat, and by self-doubt about one's capacity to address it;

2. a: propensity to inflict cruelty or acts of psychological intimidation, typically upon undeserving recipients and in a random fashion;

b: inclination to use threats and the menace of violence to keep a person or group of people in a state of intimidation and unease;

    3. a: sense that something is very, very wrong.

Example (1): "I am in a Caligulan frame of mind lately, as I notice '[e]vents begin to register / Some unwelcome forecast . . . The omens come and signs are sinister.'" **Example (2):** "I have often felt that such Caligulan 'mortifications were meant to end / At some point . . . Some hopeful hour in the past, long / Ago, but they linger, unnerving, attend / Like strange men who simply arrived one day, / Who aren't welcome to stay but won't leave.'"

From the Latin appellation Caligula

First known use 2015, USA

Summer

Barnegat Light

The gull pulls bags from trash and drags them clear.
He's big as a cat, a blur of snow and soot.
He pokes until debris spills down the pier.
He's clumsy, and somehow he's lost a foot.
Chewed off? A winter fishing line? Wedged in boards?
The stump's a small sharp spear that stings the bird
If ground is touched. He soars to foggy scree,
Alights but flaps to halfway hang in air, spurred
By pain to perform endless pirouettes.
The bay's warm surge troubles the cooler sea.
The fishing fleet returns as silhouettes.
These hours are small escapes, reprieves, rewards,
Summer the center we try to pretend
Will keep us strong, like love, and never end.

Demography

Here in the state park, we hear talk of Wal-Mart's
Amazing deals, about how well Google Maps
Displays the camping grounds. When we retire,
At sundown, firecrackers and shouts go till all hours
As tiny screens light up around the campfire
And teens roar in the communal showers.

ATV's start with a barrage of farts.
We wake, drowsy, shaken, and peer through tent flaps.
We've entered the land of Jesus, Jacuzzis,
And jet skis. Canary and cobalt, they cut the lake
Apart and send out shocks that bob the boat we sail,
Casting white sprays up from broad white asses.
We feel helpless in the gasoline breeze,
And lonely, enclosed by families with fake
Tattoos, squirt cannons, Facebook, and e-mail.
We try to read while they blast New Country.

The big guy in the neighboring tent
Sounded rude, and I wonder what he meant.
His shiny trash blows all over the grass.
I pick some up, but more comes, and it's windy.
I know we are the sum of what we choose.
They have five rowdy kids. We, none. We lose.

Scape

He's stranded in a place remote and sunless,
Wonders if, in fact, he brought himself
Here or was placed by another on this shelf,
So he rests on stone to watch the old stars turn,
Golden Pisces diving to plunge at Pegasus,
Aquarius recoiled before vast Cetus,
Lighting the ruin, and may never learn
Why he woke here or where he is, *unless* . . .

Is this an arrival or alarming return?
One stairway climbs into sheer stone.
Another drops off a cliff's verge—
Nothing to drink, and nothing to burn.
He knows only that he is left alone,
Waiting, unaided, for meaning to emerge.
Above him—undreamed, an inferno—lie
The archaic stars whose light still shapes the sky.

Sir Fish and the Bridge to Nowhere

Sir Fish dips in brackish cold
Beneath the Bridge to Nowhere,
Near the Lone Grave of Mud City,
And down the meander of Cedar Creek
Into piqued winds of Manahawkin Bay

Only to turn in again at Turtle Cove,
And be lost in muddy channels,
Follows strings of telephone poles
Leaning down over the marsh,
Sagging like ancient wash lines,

Their long chart his only landmark,
Then by luck through Log Pond Creek
At last he is returned, saved!
Weary, and hungry, a bit weepy, but happy
To be with you back at the Bridge to Nowhere . . .

Human Interest

The Cyclops gets it in the eye,
     Goliath by God's will,
And now we think the little guy
     Will always get the kill.
The nerdy girl will bag the hunk,
     The local band get big,
The kids find gold in dad's old trunk
     While grandma does a jig,
Jack—acned, stooped, and awkward—
     Trick the ancient giant,
Skinny Arthur extract the sword,
     Intern land the client,
The farmer's boy, newly knighted,
     Become the chosen one,
Ages of unfairness righted
     By a less-than-favored son,
As if, for sake of a story,
     Awful odds are annulled,
Fictions fielding hopes of glory
     Where none should be fulfilled.

Your Heroes Left You for Dead

I find I'm surprised by some happiness
As I move from a building's big shadow
Into a merciless passage of sunlight.
It annihilates the depths, distances, and angles
That define the streetscape throbbing below,
So bright it almost extinguishes sight,
But when I recognize I've been made joyful
The joy is gone, erased. I remember
Reason after massive reason to let
The moment go and yield to the tidal pull
Of thoughts that lead slowly to surrender
To the many new enemies I've not yet
Met. Friends tell me I should be *happier*,
But to think is to appreciate that even
This sunshine—brilliant, primeval balm—will burn
If I linger too long, that it can blur
A universe of details to blindness when
One stares fixedly. Should I simply turn
Away, indulge in life, raw, and its defeat,
Bask in a way fashioned from a false fire,
Or accept radiances of a desire
To stop, eyes closed, and doubtless feel the heat?

Handlers

We watch the hectic scene
Through aquarium glass
From our chilled leather seats
As if before a stage:

The baggage crew knocks
And tosses the black and blue
Bales of bulky luggage.
One absentmindedly

Kicks a folded stroller
Till it zips down a chute.
He howls a dirty joke
Over his big shoulder.

They hardly notice the weight.
They shift an endless freight
Of boxers, bras, and shoes,
Bright communion salvers

Of cosmetics, a locked
And confidential cargo
Of shampoo and compacts
Clamped stubbornly as clams.

Another flips a girl's toy case—
A pink plastic seashell—
Across a cloud canvas
From Constable. Such art!

It rides over its arc,
Across the fume-filled air,
Until it smacks and spins
Atop a growing pile.

It seems only objects—
Stiff rubber, plastic, steel—
Would survive out in
That blasted, roaring scene,

But handlers, in goggles,
Heavy gloves, and bright lime
Safety vests, shimmer
As they muscle the bags.

They thrive in the dire heat,
While we, clutching carry-ons,
Await our appalling departure
Onto overseen routes.

Black Moshannon

Pushing off, she aims upstream into bogs,
Past anglers who thread the waters with lines
For sunfish, perch, and red-finned pickerel.
She rows along the swamp of soaked logs,
A sump simmering under pines
In its vast crib of sandstone, pulls
The oars and hopes for sights of some
Ancient and rare florae evolved to trap prey,
Bladderwort or lava beard of Sundew.
Spongy peat rots the place to a humid scum.
She steers against a wind that makes her sway,
Works to keep right, scull straight, work through
Entrancing urges in the forceful sun
To surrender, to tip, to simply be done.

Siege of Fort Mifflin
(Battle of Mud Island)

A squadron of the vaunted British empire
Fell prey to mud, to wind and vengeful fire.
A ship-of-the-line ran aground and burned here,
Bombed by batteries on shore. Seeking to retire,
A sloop named Merlin stuck fast in the mire,
As Isis, Roebuck, and Pearl circled near.

Today, sparkling like swirls of fish spawn,
Undulating armadas of plastic—
Unsinkable cups, trays, strips, and bottles,
Restless, as if alive. When we are gone,
Will these tokens foretell drastic
Efforts to win new kinds of battles?

The air is heavy and wet, and I stand
Uneasily in this humid marshland.
I float in the aura of a gas giant,
Cast in its corona, watching vacant
Spacecraft cluster like trash into orbit,
Like casings of shells that failed in flight.

Mineral Point

11,000 feet

The jeep clambers through shingle and sand.
It lunges and jolts, scrums through creeks,
High to the blocked path of the mining site.
Here, floss of waterfalls spin down Holocene shapes.
These once were ancient islands, bald peaks
Rising far at sea, the ledge on which he stands
Submerged by great waves. Today, at this height,
Engelmann Spruce and Subalpine Fir spur
Old red sediment, and Krummholz, self-entwined,
Scrabbles over the timberline. What escapes
This place? Eagles arc the dark peak, confer
A smallness on all he is left to find.
Huge cumuli horde the high horizon,
And, unfinished, he can only drive back down.

Save Earth

We thought they came from distant moons.
We couldn't tell at first if they had eyes,
But we learned they have mouths. Big ones. *Good God!*
A storm of great worms squirms across the skies.
We wondered if they were loosed by ancient runes
Or slithered through some blurry dimensional door.
Then we thought *maybe earth*, that they had clawed
From a blistering crack in the seafloor.
Now we know they were planted eons ago,
Right *here*, and come to claim their rightful place.
They pour into our wrecked cities and grow.
They smash bridges, dams, and soon this very base.
They've neutralized our weapons, but we're one
Step from being saved! Behold, Mr. President,
One of these will save us. Just one, and they're done.
We're ready. We need only your permission
To deploy, and drive these things away,
But we have to do it *now, now, before they . . .*

After We Escaped the Tombs of the Blind Dead

We danced gawkily, our soles squishing
Into soggy grass at the top of the hill
In the rainstorm that night, city skyline
A cluster of crystals far off, wishing
The long song would just unspool
Forever on the kaleidoscope shrine
Of lit-up stage down below, and when we
Stopped to kiss, it never timed with the lightning,
Though we tasted the same rain on each
Other's lips, two figures one entity
In the wet darkness, in the whitening
Flash that shot through the black to reach
Us on the highest point for miles, and then
Thunder followed and we did not wonder why
With drums and applause we once again
Forgot we were supposed to die.

CASH FOR GOLD

Before you dashed with me through
Fish-scale pours of tropical storm
In the falling-down city I felt
Too long like a king of an unsettled
And marshy land, but dried in the sad
Victorian room by the sea I was better
For a while, where pink bouquet
Wallpaper shed from damp walls
Like gluey shadows in the corners
And the gold-framed painting
Over the rolled-in mattress
Was a nervous antique rash
Of silver moonlight and drenched sand.

I dreamed slowly on my side
As the restless squall billowed
The white gauze curtains
And they danced and beat all night.

In the morning, the rain went on
And a drenched seagull perched like a statue
On the next roof. We heard
Someone beyond the wall
Quarrel about money
And later heard another
In a car who laughed and whooped
About a new house and drove off.
In the noisy diner I wonder

Why we never talk about money
Until it's gone. Is it because something's
Wrong with us? Something's wrong
With us. I always knew it. I still
Love you. And look, the lights
Are turning red down the rainy avenue.

Apparition at Moss-Hanne

Ospreys orbit here, ruling as lords
Their drowned domains. We row watercourses
Through miles of lily pads, hoards
Of hemlock, spruce groves, and grim fortresses
Of alder swamp. Millions of years flood
This place, where salamanders slide in mud.
Our Depression-era log cabin warms
When we return in rain. As the storm passes,
We stir fire from damp wood. It squirms and thirsts
In muggy air, struggles up and catches barks.
The pit smokes. A winding helix of sparks
Climbs when a wet log pops and bursts
Its musty treasure of grubs to the furnace.
Above, a colonnade of oak glows and forms
Like candles on cathedral triforia.
The flames are my phantasmagoria.
Higher, a cloud, like a skull, with a grin
Too mild to scare, masks the moon. It sheers
Apart in light to frost, feather, fin—
A thing that never slows and always nears.

Autumn

Consolations of Autumn

Some are happiest when autumn comes,
Long for turning leaves, aficionados of first frost,
Put out gourds, ornamental sheaves of wheat.
They dress front porches as forsaken tombs,
Imagine themselves ghoul, zombie, and ghost,
Use kitchen knives to jab holes in sheets.
They relish mornings when windows are sheets of ice,
Yearn to don soft panoplies of scarves and gloves,
And wait all year to welcome the hard freeze
That forces birds south, woodchucks to earth, mice
To infiltrate warm cupboards, learn to love
All that leans into its finish, truly pleased
To bask in bereavement's graceful glow,
Alive in it, until it, too, must go.

Squirrel Hill

We wake to find our outdoor cat is dead.
Some drunk speeding up the block, no doubt.
The wheel's blow was so hard it spread
Her out like an old rug, rung her life out,
Speared her clavicle through the black fur,
Still lustrous, as when she was quick. She's splayed
Like a star stuck on the black sky of tar.
We feel, a moment, as if she might still stir.
But gone now, as if she never begged or played.

I scoop her tenderly as I'm able,
Our bundle of bony fur and blood—
Who posed on the porch beneath the table
As I read, lolled in the sun, left prints in mud—
Into a glossy black trash bag and carry
Her around the house to where we will bury
Her, where the yard gives way to a garbage-
Swollen gully and bare lot behind a ledge
That falls away a bit more each rainfall,

And knowing I'm nothing I scowl
At the sky, painfully blue, cold, and far,
New moon's sliver so clean it could slice me in two.
I realize, consoled, she was our dark star.
Once done, we're colored with soils and clays.
There is no more to do, so we go on, through
Our uncertain passage, through anarchic days,
Our time, and our love, too small, in past tense,
In the ever-shrinking lands beyond the fence.

The Victory Stele
of Narām-Sîn

This lecture insults the king. Is he merely
One more item to be addressed as if not
Present or no longer alive? His force
Is renewed by death. He knows what is yearly
Replanted will grow best from mud and rot,
What pours long enough returns to a source.
The surly king storms out, eager for rebirth,
Quick dawn from darkness, but this equinox
Is one of misalliance, disarray.
There is no eclipse. No magic is worth
This much. No longer the waking and long walks,
No longer the sun to etch the skies, weigh
The hours with consequence, mark the slow
End of things. Not now. His is a sour star,
A sick land, thimble ziggurats by which flow
Veins of black space, singing, and no longer far.

On Leaving an Old Mirror Out at the Curb

What do I call you at the end? Witness,
Mimic, tyrant of the departed years,
At times flatterer; others still-life, ghost,
Pure pool, twin, ludicrous door, or clearness
Leading nowhere, yet alluring as a frontier,
Great eye, roommate, spy—ominous, silent host.
Despite all you've witnessed and returned,
You recall nothing in your absolute present,
Silent movie, brittle glass bed, leaning gurney,
Knowing only what is shown, nothing learned,
What occurs but never what it has meant,
Will be, or was. Forgive this last journey
Into the earth, where you'll be bent and crack,
Where you'll shatter but be serene as stone,
Free from vanities that bathe the bone,
Razors of cold light lodged blindly in black.

Mayfair

Outside NOBU, a lone paparazzo.
No stars yet out tonight.
He wraps the camera strap
Like an archer's vambrace
To hold his Nikon in place.
Once a drummer rammed him:
They rolled on the pavement,
But no one got the shot.
Another time, a supermodel
Snapped a heel, stumbled,
Spilled her handbag on the street.
She fell on all fours, struggling
In her strapless dress to gather
Cylinders and silver cases.
Men formed a semicircle.
Flashes blazed, white like gunfire
Across her back. Her boyfriend laughed.
Tonight the photographer squats
Beside a man who begs for coins.
He watches the door, holds still, and waits.

Moose

Academy of Natural Sciences

It's been years since I first leaned upon the glass,
Left my fingerprints, craned to see past
My own reflected shape, your shoulders high
And chest a hillside, antlers an alpine pass,
Unafraid, somehow friendly, yet so vast.
You still startle, filling half the false sky.
Through my life you've stood stuffed, sad but stately.
I wanted to wander the hills and glades
Of your painted diorama. You tower
In the same black forests I've traveled lately,
And you nod, snorting, chewing a flower,
As if you never felt the hooks and blades,
And we're both, a moment, unhunted,
Unhurt in our cells, still safe, and still haunted.

Circle of the Tyrants

Unscrew the metal pegs that spur the stock.
The strings go slack and spool from courses,
Unwind and curl useless as railway track
Pulled up by an army. Embrace the neck
And swab from fret to saddle, feel forces
Vanished but yearning always to fly back.
For now, tuneless, the black body stretches
Like a swan murdered on a muddy bank,
Songless until restrung. Unleash new strings.
Pull high E to a finger joint. It etches
Small lines in skin, thin enough to kill. Still lank,
Low E, gold wound for kings, binds like a ring;
The strings are tools, tribute to horse and swan,
Till, tensed and tuned, transmuted to weapon.

Jab

I'm in the chair. Henry nimbly skims my cheek,
Like a sculptor, with an open razor.
He whispers, "See that guy, there, in the sleek
Suit, real nice, with all the rings, in Pete's chair?
He's a big boxing promoter. He owns ten
Fighters." I slowly scan the *Daily News*.
"He doesn't own them," I counter. "They're free men."
"Ah, sure he does. Ask Jimmy. He knows."

They lean to hear stories and stats, best bets,
Brazilians on the way up, weights and ages,
Promotions and perks a good fighter gets,
Big prizes, payouts, no thought of wages,
Objects of rumor from Philly and Cleveland,
Kept like big cats, cherished, giants from Ukraine,
Prospects pegged, from Peru and England,
Sparring to get back fees advanced in pain.

Watchers

Quis custodiet ipsos custodes

1.

No longer three. Tonight we see just two,
Who loiter and seem to watch us below
From the street—vaguely framed by the window
Like a spy photo—*there*, in the lamplight.
For weeks now, I've counted and there were three,
But I'm almost certain that just last night,
And again tonight, there are only two.
It's better, now that you've come to join me.
It's easier with two sets of eyes to see
What's really been going on out there.
Together we make an effective pair.
It's safer this way. Right? It is. Yes . . . Yes.
It's now two to two when they watch us,
And no third, not now, now that I have you.

2.

You see the two, the two that linger there?
        Of course. They're always standing there.
And you? Where were you before you came here?
        Around. You know. All around here . . .
It's hard to make out much about those men.
        Oh, no, I think you've got it wrong.
Got what wrong? You told me. Tell me again.
        Not men. I've known that much all along.

Not men? They're surely not women. Oh, no.
        Not women and not men, I say.
You talk, but I can't understand a word.
        I try to fix my focus, but they stay blurred.
What do we watch? What watches us below?
        Two things from very far away.

3.

I dropped awake and felt it was a dream,
Or seemed to be. I dreamed our prey
Was waiting, just like us, for something too.
When you watch a thing, what you seem
At night to see, or what it seems by day,
Adjusts, and doubts, like enemies, accrue.
And when the watchers watch each the other
They're too busy, and never pause to think
Of what occurs in the time it takes to blink,
Or that both might be watched by another.

Dominion of the Parthians

University of Pennsylvania Museum
of Archaeology and Anthropology

The iridescent maps along the walls
Reveal lost empires that spread like species
Overbred toward their final decline;
The halls adorned with masks and dolls
Of nations destroyed by war and disease,
And fulcra on which bored queens would recline,
The marble busts of conquerors, satyr
Poised over a pool, a restyled colonnade,
Charms for love and health, onyx amulets,
Cuneiform incised in clay from Ur,
Galleries glamorous with gold and jade
Once gathered by war, too much to possess,
All seem to slip from me, become less true,
Now less to me than sitting here with you
And seeing that what little we've done
And all we have will just as well be gone.

Total Wrecks

1.

So pass a glass and pour the bourbon round.
Sip the smoke that shines a tarnished crown.

2.

We love the way the roasted waves embalm
Our Cyclops figurehead: It dives toward the calm
That claims us, before the black that follows blue.

3.

We're run-through, demasted, ghosts for crew,
Though we plead for some rest at last, some sleep
In an ancient plot, among familial ranks
Of prouder dead, or seafloors freshened with plunder.

4.

Ornate galleons, we list in the squall, roll down
To unload our cargoes into the deep,
Spreading sparks of coins, canvas, ribs, and planks.
On lower decks, the cannons that once thundered
Are cooled, and all the filthy gunners drowned.

Kingdom of the Spiders

It's pitch black and pissing down so hard
You see nothing but tearful shards of light.
You start to feel like your life's an anchor
In a wet box. Lift it. The ATM's bright
Screen beeps, pitiless, displays a message for
Insufficient Funds, and spits the plastic card
Back out with a click. The songs you believed
Were ugly or stupid have grown beautifully
In you, because you have, too. The modest
House in which you slept, where you received
Junk mail, what you kept and dutifully
Cleaned and considered your own address
Is theirs, of course. You knew that all along.
Such mortifications were meant to end
At some point, magically on some birthday,
Some hopeful hour in the past, long
Ago, but they linger, unnerving, attend
Like strange men who simply arrived one day,
Who aren't welcome to stay but won't leave.
Nothing will grow better or go right, it seems,
But you can still cling to some comfort.
It will end. Not soon. Eventually.
Your love weeps all night. At dawn, she screams.
You can't know what designs more pain might bring.
Cold streets fill with crowds. You want to fight.
You spit and shout. In daydreams you sing.

Insomnia Redux

The house creaks, as if alive, and outside
Recycling bins rattle—magnifiers

Of underlying silence. The hour proves,
Again, she lacks whatever sleep requires.

The black seems to change, but moves
As only one darkness, with her inside.

She prods his back to see if he's asleep,
But he's out. She can't understand why,

But she can't stop thinking of the basement,
The little room almost closed with clutter deep

In winter earth, cold even in July,
Where they store Christmas ornaments,

Halloween costumes, Easter decorations.
She rises, pulls her slippers on, thinking *the floors*

Will be cold, and descends a staircase,
Then another, thinking of compensations

That keep her close to him, closing doors
As she goes, as if partly to erase

What falls behind her, switching on
Every light, till the house is bright

As a cruise ship stranded on the dark hill.
She pauses in the kitchen to open

A drawer, then down to the last place to light
The bare bulb in the basement. *What a thrill,*

To light the house as if it burns.
Then she pulls the breaker and the house goes

Black . . . He wakes, feels for her but can't find her.
The flashlight's bewildering beam turns

Through the house, casting a harp of shadows
Up the wall through the back of a chair,

Scaring off a cat, but she's nowhere,
And he has to get the house lit again,

So he keeps on, room to room, until
He's in the basement, and there,

In the small circle of light, breaker box and main.
He sees someone, kneeling and weirdly still,

Slumped doll-like, hair shrouding face.
It rises, slowly, and he's relieved it's she,

And then, confused, sees it's not she at all.
Somehow, how, he can't tell, she's taken his place,

Behind a mask that looks like . . . could it be,
Like *his* face, and he's backed to the icy wall,

And then she lifts the blade to him as she
Pleads through the slit hole of mouth *"Please help me."*

Caligulan

Your bank calls. Events begin to register
Some unwelcome forecast. The dreamy nurses
Switch to *Goodfellas* on the overhead TV.
The omens come and signs are sinister.
Texts go unreturned. You're out of coffee.
The Olympian Jupiter curses.
In sleep, a great toe kicks you back to earth.
The slaves stage a play about the Under-
World. The smoke alarm fails, and your computer crashes.
Your favorite gladiator is lashed
For theft, lightning blackens your temple, thunder
Sinks your song, because, like the day of birth,
The day you'll wake and have your death is set,
But just hasn't, just hasn't happened yet.

Winter

Funeral Insurance

We do not rhyme much anymore,
      Yet here we are—a pair.
We hardly ever get to the store,
      And find it hard to care.

We're fixed here in our tiny home,
      The stair-chair stuck half way,
The blinds cocked, sofa seeping foam,
      Neighbors long moved away.

At times, we can't stand each other,
      Too slow, too uncertain to run
Off or start with another,
      So, together, we're done.

It's years since we were really young,
      But now we're really old,
Ancient as our house, which sits unsold,
      Doorbell and phone unrung,

Me, cold and unrecorded as snow
      That fell at sea, and you,
A flight, first listed overdue,
      Then lost, long, long ago.

Hotel Water Deemed Safe Despite Corpse

Some dawns, you want to hide on the far side
Of the sun. Your flank's staved in, reserves spent,
Mercenaries in revolt. At least that's how it feels.
Ill warnings lap all night in the tide.
Other news too. Rancid smells steam from a vent.
You can only wait for what a day reveals,
One more hour awash in trivial terrors.
Storms come together to make this weather,
Which, though bad, like us, won't stay here long.
You need to get control, make no errors.
You need to focus. You need to stay strong.
When someone dies, there's a lot of work to do.
You need to pull yourself together.
No time for distractions or to ask why or who.

Entertainment Destination

Bethlehem, Pennsylvania

Behold the black and idle cage. The ore-crane
Is now adorned with Sultanic neon: <u>*SANDS*</u>.
It lures locals from hills to heated halls.
The great grim arm that veered to bear
Titanic loads of fresh-cooled steel to trains
That coursed corridors to cities back east—
Raising kingdoms beside the sea—now stands
Dormant, a bough from petrified bole that gains
No more from rain or earth. Inside are feasts.
The rooms are gloom and plush. Jackpots ring
And flash like a childhood amusement pier,
To calm the flush from wins that run to worries:
When riskers exile themselves from these lanes
Through sliding doors, the sky fills up with cries
That strike the ear as odd, so far from surf, and wings
Of gulls that float and wait above the walls.

Unlorded

Behind us all an ancient king gone blind,
Who gropes at books, beside a queen who's lost
Her once-worshiped beauties, her taunting songs,
And all her appetites, save that for sleep.
Conceits as well have dimmed, lost hawk and hind,
And what was spent is only felt as cost.
They find they hear no more the wind that long
Ago propelled their fields to drought, put sheep
Into the earth, when rainfall loosened soil,
And, if they still recall our names and days
We took the games and shook the eaves with roars,
And laughed until we were emptied of breath,
They know we carried with us hurt and toil,
And voyaged far to get where flocks could graze,
Found humor, even happiness, in wars,
And kindness, as well, and life, in kind, in death.

Ice Dwellers Watching
the Invaders

The ship is locked beneath frozen mountains.
       It crunches by inches against white floes.
Its masts are bare cold poles of long-stripped tents,
       Its silhouette a stalagmite, its rows

Of furled sails, half-mast, sagging like bellies
       Over the black pedestal of the hull.
Five seals splash and plunge near the icy shore.
       Tubes of blood and blubber, they oar

The arctic waters, float in the ship's reflection
       As it leans and groans on the frozen
Depths. In its dark hold are harpoons, clubs, one gun.
       Snow that took the color of the late sun

Just as easily accepts its absence.
       Nothing seems to happen. A polar bear
Is unconcerned with the peculiar presence.
       Nothing would dare challenge

       The terrible essence of his deadly kingdom.
       What could kill more easily? And what for?

Dishwasher

He washes dishes in the dawn,
       Though really, still, it's dark.
The light has yet to slice through drawn
       Draperies on a shark-

Shaped pizza cutter and blue-whale
       Ice-cream scooper. The spoons
And forks, bright knives, ring like chain mail
       In the soapy lagoon,

The arsenal of cutlery,
       The spider-eggy fluff
That clings like mold to crockery,
       And other hardened stuff,

The dots of dusty plum that blot
       The stems that held the wine,
Like bloody sprays of those who fought
       And died along a line,

A puncture in the vinyl glove
       Leaks in dishwater—
And she still sleeps two floors above—
       As stacked saucers totter.

In corners are shards, diamonds uncut,
       Kaleidoscopic, and sauce
Across the ceiling, chips that jut
       From rug and couch, all tossed

Like remnants of an old battle,
       An ancient, raging rerun,
When fists made the tables rattle
       And no one recalls who won.

February Song

The brash knell of an angry bell choir, clangs
Of a belfry at the height of a hurricane,
Or just a trolley pronouncing its next stop—
She works to fix a worn-out wind chime, hangs
It by a finger so it tolls a haphazard refrain,
All gongs and happy ringing, then lets it drop,
Its song abruptly cut off with a clatter.
It makes me wonder what remaining detours
We have before the end. I do not know
Much, or understand the things that matter,
But this dawn I want to learn. Out-of-doors
A thin rain fastens banks of last night's snow
With ice, sealing soft powder into steel
Casings, freezing a million shapes to one,
Like the memories that make us, and I
Am failing too, like the light that already feels
As if it's fading before the small sun
We can't see has even climbed the sky.

Atlantica

At a touch, the pane of ice jigsaws, cracks
To diamond scatter, hard cold clouds
Clustered against a mountain chain.
One large shard holds its shape, tracks
Its slow starfish way down the windshield, crowds
Out ever smaller nicks of ice. The rain
Will soon steal its contours, but for a while
It is my continent, rhododendron,
Moth wing, milk spill, embryo, no Atlantis
Or Antarctica, but a sunken isle
I've named *Atlantica*, frozen cauldron
Filled with snowstorms, a far home, locked atlas,
Fighting to recall the word and reclaim
Myself from a place that has taken my name.

Queen of the Demonweb Pits

The deal feels wrong. Feeling's gone. Or has it?
Are you holding or are you holding out?
At this frantic hour, what can a word mean?
Would you stay so you can do one more hit
Or take the last bag, safe in your pocket,
To lock up back in your apartment unseen
And alone . . . no, you stay with those who can't
Stop pacing and talking again and again through
The same stories—are they the same stories?—
Now that the heavy curtains won't keep slants
Of aspiring light out, and the things you
Said are said by another, and worries
Snare your mind in a wire tangle of too quick
Thought quickly thought and quickly thought again,
Because left alone or leaving you will greet old fears.
So you stab at a smile but you're getting sick,
Then an eerie half-sight—at dawn as a child
You woke and stepped out and took in—oh, years
Of buried embarrassments start to flow—
But no—there is the sunlight where you stepped,
Bright as a supernova on the new snow
Where you curled up in white so soft you slept.

Between Sides Seven and Eight of *Die Walküre*

STEREO OSA-1509, London, FFrr

The time between a side is like a tide
Of silence between epochs, the stereo
A small shrine concealed in a black alpine
Bergschrund beneath snow-white blinds that hide
The ceremony's indigo vacuum-tube glow.
Silence is always the source of the Rhine.
Brushing off dust, stray hairs, remnants of life,
Brief interval in the deeps—between the blows
Of hunters' horns that summon blood-red light,
Cold trills that instill a chill of coming strife—
Tender rise of the silver arm: the stylus, slow
As seasons, lowers its blade . . . and the flight
Stirs from the night the descending daughters
And glides and sings upon the black waters.

Judgement

Bonnie's Roxx, Atco, New Jersey, 1990

O, our expressions grim, so serious!
And menacing, as if we're benching weights
Or gravely working at a car's engine.
We strive to seem mysterious
And sometimes truly entered altered states,
Burned up with rude bolts of adrenaline.
The drums command the stage like big black guns
Upon a fortress. Dwarfed by Marshall stacks,
We swing our greasy hair like myrmidons
Thrashing at rival columns. Ten hot suns
Assembled above make steam of sweat, axe
And archery, broadsword, emblem, and bronze
Armor. We swarm in smoke, crude ghosts, chthonic,
Striving, one solstice, to make ourselves mythic.

Broad and Washington

New Year's Day, Mummers

An awkward spin unbends into a strut
As sequined brawlers grin, gavotte, and stray,
Ominous jesters whose frolic survives
Obscure origins. Bejeweled banjos jut
And swipe in rude chevrons of bawdy play,
Partly primitive but also casually contrived.
Confetti clings like pollen to avenues
Governed by this throng—whose skits and prances
Proclaim them preservers of contrary motion:
Gowned brigades of misrule, bright mob that skews
Its way through regally drunken dances,
Risen from an empire sunk in the ocean
To foam over the city, stir chaotic chords,
Adored and mad, our disorderers and lords.

Penrose Diner

New Year's Day

By dawn, the year's emptied out, exhausted.
Stadiums dock like freighters in the fog,
But one well-lit stronghold never locks its doors.

Here, nothing will end or start. Through frosted
Windows, we watch a red, three-legged dog
Roll in the cold street, happy. Abandoned stores
Announce they once sold CHRIS[TM]AS ORNAMENT[S].
The waitresses smell of fresh laundry
And menthol cigarettes, arrive with winks
Like busy nurses. All around is cement,
And there's a hotel in a lot filled with debris.

His cheek's a slug along the glass. "You think
Anyone's been found dead in there?" he says.
She sips slowly at scalding coffee, "oh, *yes*."

For Lynn, At Lake Nockamixon

1.

Gunshots go off in threes somewhere across
The water. Unreal as stage-side thunder

They still sound another unwelcome
Signal, to remind us of new loss

On an otherwise quiet day. We wander
Through a thousand pines lately succumbed

To wind or water, pressed flat on the hill
Like grass on which a body lay, shallow

Root beds pulled up. They've become frilled flowers
Caked ghostly with crumbling white earth. The tranquil

Sounds of the lake are like sleep, and fallow
As the fields we sit for what feels like hours

In an old duck blind, at ease on thatched thrones
Of straw and soil, flattering ourselves we're simple

As the whistle of wind and waves that bring
Songs as they discard themselves onto stones.

2.

Deer panicked last night in the cold scalpel
Of our headlights, swiftly disappearing.

Like them, we were startled, and we were lost.
Half of them are dead by now, one day on,

The others driven away. The partnered shrieks
Of blue jays in the bare trees accosted

Us in the forbidding December dawn,
Alarming us from troubled sleep like creaks

Of doors not opened in years, harsh cries
Not anarchic but made to mimic hawks,

Even mock simple human sentences,
Counterpoint, crescendo, coda, reprise.

3.

At the fortress dam, we step onto the docks,
So many starlings in the trees they crowd our senses

Till there is nothing else. A lonely
Melody escapes the multitudinous ferment,

Then blends into the din again, lone
But never unaccompanied, or only

A trick of our ears, and what it meant
Or might have meant is just as quickly flown.

4.

We work our way along the barren shore,
Hiking through thorns to a flooded quarry.

A northern harrier floats high overhead,
A mote in winter clouds, making her kingdom.

We below must learn ways to speak, to design,
Serve, and remember, each of us no more

Than a conduit of kindness and crime, worry
And wish. The hawk's beauty seems almost a sign

That nothing kills more than it creates,
Or is wrong with what we finally become.

The unpredictable sun surges
And fades through quickening clouds. Trees lean

And then resume their full heights, briefly freed
From the impatient wind's unending urges.

We recline on the sloping meadow, difficult mates,
Watching the light change, watching it recede

On the black water below, where, unseen,
Silver carp and the deeper catfish feed.

5.

We await the hawk's eventual descent,
A small portion of the world's endless hunt

And hunger. How is it we can go through
Our lives without being routed or sent

To madness, wild with all we want,
And filled to vastness with all we view?

We hear the far guns go off again,
Their echoes growing louder on the lake.

6.

The hawk drops until she's lost from sight.
Though reluctant to leave the glen,

We stand, wipe dirt from our hands, and start to make
Our way, but linger to behold another flight:

Gangs of brittle sycamore leaves, buoyant forms
Sharp at their margins, stir in wind, urge and yield

Like big flocks of birds, borne aloft, as one,
On sustaining currents, go up in restless swarms,

Rising, and our eyes follow them, and we shield
Our faces, and wince as they enter the sun.

Spring

Kite

I ran my kite till it gulled at the sun,
And from the newfound flight it took
Command as much as I, and trained
My arm toward the sky, and strained
The armature of spreaders, spar, and knock.
It threw its silhouette against the sun,
Then bowed blue before a berm of cloud,
And set itself against a greater blue.
It swooped, twisted my wrists, and grew
To be too strong, as nervy as a bird
Of prey, a winged but featherless
Raptor I once held, now spun
Away and unbearable to possess,
A thing apart; though still tethered,
Fatherless, and finally unfathered.

Day in the Park

The helpers sweep remains of past events,
Banks of crushed paper cups, banana peels,
Broken tape. Bored, they go about their chore,
And make the park the way it was before
The "Zombie Fun Run." No point being dull
When waging war on a disease that kills.
The Good Humor truck was once an ambulance.
You can tell. It's shaped oddly like a skull.
It's spring but cold. An ice-cream cone brings chills.
Dog shit piles up in bags or sticks to heels.
Along the pier men slouch and fish for eels.
A navy destroyer, widowed by war,
Waits with its Ghost Fleet, rocks faintly in its berth.
The wind blows more trash. No one thinks of death.

Visible Spectrum

Daffodils, two of them, astonish me,
Ambushing me from winter's nowhere
And nothing, between tectonically separated
City sidewalk rammed up by an oak tree's
Roots and the rumbling blur of a street, heir
To compost of last year's leaves, decorated
By the locust shells of Trojans and Nestlé's.
The green stems bend with the bright Easter weight
Of the bulbs, richer than yolks, stronger than sunlight,
Swaying portentously in the warm breeze.
Hidden in their hoods like crayon cobras, they wait
With lamprey maws. Then another strange sight
From my window, the Cherry Blossom,
Only yesterday a skeletal display,
Now shines like sunset on miles of snow,
And I am relieved. Spring tallies its sum.
Light on a white patch of wall at mid-day
Reminds me to hang something there, though
I don't know what, but it's been a full year
Or longer I've meant to do it, and yet
I've done nothing, or done so much else I forgot.
No. Three years. Can it be? Four? Fear
Starts to get the best of me, an old debt
Ignored and climbing. Equations will work out
To conclusions, whatever they may be.
By afternoon, one of the daffodils is dead,
Torn and stomped apart by a passing kid.
I float in the mystery of a tranquil

Red-shift, an unending afternoon, always
Away from an unknown source, arguing I'm free,
That I can stay here and all else, ablaze,
Must turn about me just to keep me still.

At the Florida
Antiquarian Book Fair

The dealers slump in book-lined booths. They send
Sentiments from new iPhones and laptops,
Ignoring the volumes in which they are penned.
Crowds slouch in sandals and shorts, but a few attend
Dressed as dandies or flappers, pose for photo ops,
Admire Art Deco, post for Facebook friends.

Out the big ballroom doors the noon sun stuns
For a moment, then, from the hot blur
Come telephone wires slung like old tendons
Among buildings declared Historic, that once
Meant much, now merely preserved, patched with plaster,
Marked with plaques of crooners, felons, tycoons . . .

Above, contrails cross clouds, and a black fly
Swims in the deep and disorderly sky.

Light Illumined

Mentre che sì per l'orlo, uno innanzi altro,
Ce n'andavamo, e spesso, il buon maestro
Diceami: "Guarda: giovi ch'io ti scaltro'

Wind conveys a muffled tune from a truck
Up from the valley, and they make out
Eddie Money's "Two Tickets to Paradise"
Under the crinkle of plastic bags stuck
In the trees. The wind goes on, and all's doubt.
The strong sun lights up thin ditches of ice.
They can't know how long anything will last,
But this winter has held on far too long,
Overhanging spring, squeezing them with suspense,
Suspicious that something is really wrong,
Keeping them, against their hopes, in the past.
They pick their way through marshy ground. Dense
Shadows stretch out in late sunlight as they
Gain the rising hillside of cut-down stalks
And desiccated cobs. He goes ahead
Of her, determined for the top, to see
If there is anything to view. She walks
More slowly her own way, never led
Or leading. The world is made, for a moment,
Of mud, bent stems, debris of harvested crops.
Below, silos and bare groves gather
Along the stream. Ending his ascent,
He turns to her at the top and she drops
Into the horizontal sunlight like a bather
Going under a western ocean at sunset.
The sun, almost unbearable by now

In its last minutes brands her to a dark
Shape enclosed by baffling glare and pure jet
Of haloed light, like the last of a bough
At a bonfire's core that still casts off sparks,
And he looks too long trying to see her,
The brightness bent over millions
Of miles, cold carried by its brilliance,
And before he can blink it makes her disappear.

The Gelding

Wind warms aromas of manure and hay.
In the barn's cool shade, a stallion's sedated,
Secure for now in his familiar stall,
Stamping softly, disposed to obey
His handler's stroke and tender call.

The years since he broke his maiden, ruled
The sunny roar of the post parade,
Have been one long break from the gate, lulled
By fame, by days kept, by seconds rushed,
By hours reared, centuries strode and played,

By grooms rubbed, jockeys rode, entirely in thrall.
He sees and thinks of nothing but the wall.
His scrotum is slit, spermatic cord crushed.
The vet keeps the slick red shape, ornate with veins,
That could be mistaken for an infant.

The horse will never pull wildly again at reins,
Slower now, serene, soon to forget all he can't
Sense, can't do, won't know, no longer want,
The infinite urges, taken, will never again taunt
Him. Farm dogs whine and plead, scratch and pant

At the gate, knowing what they will get.
The man holds the flaccid, bulging wet
Shape up to shine in the sun a moment
Over the slobbering jaws, then drops it.
The dogs scrabble on loose gravel and tear

The discarded sop among them till their
Jaws are lit with blood, muzzles slick with sperm.
They rove off, rowdy, rewarded, to rule the farm,
To revel, having seized their rightful prize,
Attended by adoring swarms of eager flies.

Equinoctial

A Yuengling bottle stands sentinel
Inside a rusted *Philly Weekly* box. A wet page
Wallpapered to one side shows a grinning man,
Wicked gleam in eyes almost illegible.
He's posed, oiled and flexed, as if on a stage,
Above frozen pizza crust, a crumpled Coke can.
It's rain, then snow, rain again, the slush black
With exhaust and tar, and the city slides
Evilly through the hard, final assault
Of winter's long offensive. Spring will be back,
Or so we're told, though oddly overdue, like tides
Gone out and not come back, and, everywhere, salt.
The seasons glue down, pull off painfully,
Like memories that stay in the eyes from dreams
A moment, mazelike, before they're rubbed out.
Something is wrong. Something has rudely
Changed around us, or in us, unsewn seams,
Or gorging rain before killing drought.

Results

We are the ones who box the picks,
Superstitiously select each day
A birth hour or star sign, or random array.
We gladly invite this *tax*

On the unwise, on the *desperate*,
Because we feel as if we're trapped
By snares laid that long ago snapped
Shut on us. We're held with debt

That ankles us. We try to thrive,
Caught in jobs we hate all week,
Return to costly houses at night, contrive
By all means to twist free. So we seek

A way out. It's easier to lose
Alongside millions, a promise small
As a speck, almost impossible
To believe. On top of what we choose,

What we spend and try to save,
It's always there. It's what we have.

Meridian

9,000 feet

We trek the steep rim
Past shrunken orange
Strip of dead fox, still bright,

Luring flies.
The lake is long, a loose wound
In the mountain's chest.

Stripped, we douse
Hike-hot skin
In ancient black,

The dark mud plush
To first careful steps,
Sting of sinking in—

Then we float out
Over the secret floor
Where arctic deeps purl beneath

And vast forces forged
A hidden foundation
Millions of years before.

My white hand melts into murk,
Urging swarms of froth
To rise and hiss

On the surface.
My Iron Age limbs scull
The tingling cold.

Clouds bruise the high pines.
A hawk rounds back alone,
Persistent in Spartan circles.

In-School Suspension

We sweated and dozed like barbarians
In a deer-hide tent at the height of spring's
Roasting heat, crowded in for various
Affronts, crimes, and faults. When one among us

Was handed, from the disciplinarian's
Office, a pink paper slip, listing things
He'd done that were deemed truly nefarious
(To us hilarious) and saying he was

Expelled altogether from school, he heaved
The heavy 1950s stapler from
Our minder's desk and hammered the paper
To his head. The first two staples rebounded

And clicked on the tiles. We were almost relieved
When the third clinched, pressed deeper by his thumb,
And seized subcutaneous hold. This caper
Did it: We were, for once, astounded.

With the form draped over one eye, he smiled
For us, turning slowly in the humidity,
A satanic clown, our own Spartacus
For a sparkling second we won't forget.

We roared and roared in our hot galley, piled
Up laughs till they hid any stab of pity.
We all knew he wouldn't even be missed
As, clutched by the wrist, he loosed one last threat

And was hauled from the room and the door boomed
Shut. We never saw him again. One by one,
We turned our faces downward and resumed,
With the dust he'd raised churning in the sun.

Mother's Day

She stalks the May yard,
Mewing for her kittens,
Two black like her,
Under the slanted iron fence,
Toward the ravine behind,
Crammed with bald tires
And the dull fires of tangled
Wire rusted into bonnets.

The orphaned crown of a bird's nest,
Torn from our eave
By a storm, lays a wrecked knot
Of twine and twig in the gutter.

On the cracked porch
The remaining slivers
Of a broken mirror glint where
The brush missed them
Last season.

The mother moves
Like a shadow along the edges
Of the yard, a helpless curl
Of fur in her jaws.

Cryptid

The water gives nothing back. A child squeals
"Where's the monster?" She's jubilant
But braced impatiently for disappointment.

I track the peat-blackened surface but glimpse
Nothing in its fossil depths, just froth
From screws that churn the loch to cola fizz.

We chug toward the coral reaches of the castle,
Hugged by mountains, buoyed on the abyssal trench,
Oil-bath sheen all around. Saurian cumuli

Lumber down the sky. Hidden in the black, I know,
Lurk centuries of eel, char, and fanged pike,
But where is our monster, the one we thought

Would always be there somewhere, though hidden?
The tiny girl in pink stamps her silver slippers.
No monster today, or ever. I catch the shallow

Smudges of my face in the cabin window.

Easter

The smoky dawn lights miles of Jersey sludge.
The route I take toward the ancient church
Is forsaken, more so than I remembered—
Lots for sale, blocks to let, and what won't budge:
Old liquor stores, strip clubs, and miles of marsh.
A song revives me after I've entered.
Still, I sag inside my chalk-striped suit of ash,
With pink at neck, a body in a bog,
Pressed down in dark by centuries of soil.
Lilies massed at altar will soon be trash.
Weak light strains through stained glass as if in fog.
Bouquets become weed beds. I'm pearl and shell,
A cur cast off and far from pit and throne,
From dawn and dearth, from brother, ghost, and son.

Who Is He Dares Enter These My Woods

I'm late for work. I can't figure what's wrong
At first, but then I feel the peaceable kingdom
That the daily rush-hour leaves in its wake.
I hail Miss Bonnie, who's puffed as an autumn
Woodchuck in her billowing brand-new plum
Summer dress, offer her my arm, and take
Her bag. She sighs "my knees are bad today"
As I help her into the van that takes her
To the museum. At the trolley-stop,
An elegant, antique gentleman sways
Slightly to and fro in the pollen-soaked air,
Tapping his cane on the gum-stippled blacktop,
Blind behind big black plastic glasses.
He smiles, so I do too, and then I steer
Him to the trolley steps and find myself a seat.
University students off to noon classes
Climb on, more at each stop, unkempt, sincere,
Slumping in public pajamas, entering Tweet
And text to slim slabs of cheerful light.
At Fifteenth I'm off and up the stairs.
Oldenburg's season-streaked Clothespin
Is an obelisk in its imperial height,
Brooding over a day's urgent affairs
And remorseless commerce, and I wander,
Timeless, in a Pliocene daze until I spot her
On colonial cobblestones, a glint

Of recognition, a wave, and, surprised,
I clumsily reach to embrace her, skin
Cold as clouds, and without a hint
Of hesitation she holds the embrace, eyes
Neptune blue, still thin as a flamingo—I
Feel her spine, serrated under my palms, so odd
To see her here with me in the future,
One more suddenly-woken creature.
We laugh, but it's already later than
I know, and as I try to whisper goodbye
A rancid garbage truck's long sauropod
Snore drowns me out and the mounting sun
Breaks into a crown, vast and intimate,
Like an ending eclipse—a bright instant
Over tall buildings, a distant cool flare
Makes me clamp my eyes shut in the infinite
Noise and forfeiture of spring and I forget,
For an uncertain step, how on earth I got here.

The Author

Ernest Hilbert's debut collection *Sixty Sonnets* (2009) was described by X.J. Kennedy as "maybe the most arresting sequence we have had since John Berryman checked out of America." His second collection, *All of You on the Good Earth* (2013), has been hailed as a "wonder of a book," "original and essential," an example of "sheer mastery of poetic form," containing "some of the most elegant poems in American literature since the loss of Anthony Hecht." Hibert works at Bauman Rare Books in Philadelphia, where he lives with his wife, Lynn Makowsky, Keeper of the Mediterranean Section at the University of Pennsylvania Museum of Archaeology and Anthropology.

www.ingramcontent.com/pod-product-compliance
Lightning Source LLC
Chambersburg PA
CBHW020509100426
42813CB00030B/3178/J